To Ferndale School

My Kids
Bubbles and Bubbly

DUCK AS A THIRD LANGUAGE

Nelly Julchen Rempel

Nelly Julchen Rempel

FriesenPress

Suite 300 - 990 Fort St
Victoria, BC, Canada, V8V 3K2
www.friesenpress.com

Copyright © 2015 by Nelly Julchen Rempel
First Edition — 2015

Photography by Helmut Rempel
and Nelly Julchen Rempel

All rights reserved.

No part of this publication may be reproduced in
any form, or by any means, electronic or mechanical,
including photocopying, recording, or any information
browsing, storage, or retrieval system, without
permission in writing from the publisher.

ISBN
978-1-4602-6446-1 (Paperback)
978-1-4602-6447-8 (eBook)

1. Nature, Animals, Birds

Distributed to the trade by The Ingram Book Company

Dedication

I dedicate this book to my family, especially to my Mom, Lisa, who got stuck with caring for my little pets, and my brother Helmut who helped me with some of the sightings and took many of the interesting photos.

Nelly Rempel
Nov. 29, 2014

Imprinting is a unique form of bonding, in which a very young animal fixes its attention on the first object with which it has visual or auditory experience, and then follows that object. In nature the object is usually mother. Imprinting has been studied mostly only in chickens, ducks, and geese, but a comparable form of learning apparently occurs in the young of many mammals and some fishes and insects.

In ducklings, mallard, and domestic chicks, imprinting can be accomplished in a few hours, but receptivity to imprinting stimuli vanishes at the age of about 30 hours.

The Story of BUBBLES

It was June 27, 1978 and I was peddling my bike back to the house, from an excursion to our bush. There I had gathered some mosses and British Soldiers for a wood land terrarium scene. My brother, Helmut, who was mowing hay, signaled to me to come to him. "I've had an accident", he said. There, exposed by the cut grass, was a mound of feathers which concealed about 13 pale blue eggs, and a duck's foot. How Mother duck got away from the mower, I still cannot understand. Some of the eggs were severely crushed, but others only cracked. Helmut informed me that two young foxes had been looking for the nest and were right now in the hedge just a short distance away.

I hurried off for a dish. When I entered the house with, "Mother, I haven't had a pet for a long time!" Mother's face kind of paled as all my previous pets flashed through her mind – a weasel, a blackbird, two robins, Wally the raccoon, King a red-tailed hawk, etc., and now what!

She was stuck feeding them during the day while I was away at work.

Competition was stiff. As I was returning, I heard Helmut make a commotion: the Kits were very close to the nest. I took 8 eggs where the chicks still seemed alive, and left the crushed eggs for the foxes.

Now what? Since the eggs were cracked, I felt I had no choice but to "hatch" them although they still had some of the yellow egg sac unabsorbed. I put them in a box under my plant light and covered them with a piece of glass. I wanted to keep the moisture in so that the chicks would not dry to the egg shell. I had opened the shells only partly.

In the morning, there were 3, live, wet ducklings. I put them in a dry box, again with the light for warmth. Did you ever see anyone or anything do the "Montreal Jog". Jogging on one spot, for 3 days? They would just not settle nor eat. Two chicks died.

Hamburg 1970

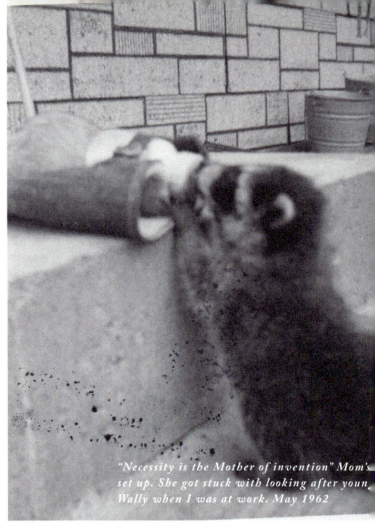

"Necessity is the Mother of invention" Mom's set up. She got stuck with looking after young Wally when I was at work. May 1962

Our pet King, turned out to be a female Red-Tailed Hawk. She was domesticated and got lost in a storm, and now lived at the neighbours, who fed her bologna. She often came to visit us, here she got raw beef. One day Mom and I went shopping. When we got home Mom asked Dad were the steaks were which she put out to thaw. "Oh, King was here begging."

Then I changed my strategy. I took an old wool sweater and a mason jar full of warm water and wrapped the duckling alongside. We both compromised – she settled and sat ON the jar – I raised the ceiling!

The morning after I got the eggs I had to start to work early, and as I drove by the field, I saw a duck alight in the nest area. Had it been the weekend, I would have put the ducklings back in the nest and sat in the hedge – probably with the foxes, to see if mama duck would consider the offer.

Well, this little duckling decided she was stuck with me, and she might as well make the best of it. We named her "Bubbles" Her first swim was a disaster. Did you ever see a wet duck? I did! She was very demanding, always wanting a baby sitter.

For the first 2 weeks, I always kept her confined when we did not have the time to be with her in the yard. According to her, I was her mother, and no one else in the family counted, although I could not see a striking resemblance.

The first time we let her outside without supervision, she hung around for a while and then disappeared. My Mother looked and called but to no avail. At 3 p.m. she arrived home. The second day, she did the same thing, Mother called her, no response. When I came home at 5:30, I called and she came waddling through the garden, telling me all about her exciting day.

I felt that if she was going to orientate herself, she needed more freedom. Initially, she followed me like an elastic. She was never more than a foot behind me. She was RIGHT behind me. I felt I could have used a fly's eye. I would be hoeing, pulling weeds, etc.and she would snuggle up to me, sit down and 'bubble' in the soil, with her beak. Everything was checked in this manner, grass, sticks, toes, etc.

We fed her Turkey Starter as the feed dealer suggested.

Then she got to be teen age. She would stay about 6 feet from me and be very proud of her independence. When she was 3 weeks old, I went on a 2 week vacation. When I returned, to my great surprise, she was extremely excited to see me. She came running to me with her beak open, and her wings spread. She was now about three quarters grown and in full adult female mallard plumage. She looked lovely with her distinct spectrum on the wings.

The beautiful wing spectrum of the mallard duck.

When she reached adult size, she made no attempt to fly. Well, since I was her mother, it was up to me to teach her. Soooo, first glancing up and down the road to make sure the "coast was clear", I took off (on the ground) running down the driveway, flapping my "wings'". I ran just fast enough for her to not be able to keep up with me with her waddling. She would fly, and be air born approximately 2 feet off the ground. If I took her for a walk, that is exactly what it was. She would never fly, she would walk. My brother felt she was the furthest walking duck in the world. (I'll have to check the Guinness Book of Records for that.)

After 2 weeks of vacation and some rain, the lawn needed cutting. By the way, every time I wanted to get to the car, I had to sneak out of the front door, because Bubbles patrolled the back door. I did manage to get to the garage and the riding lawn mower. I have this habit of singing or humming. (Once I did it in the geography class many moons ago, until the teacher suggested I quit!) So, not giving it a second thought, and with all that noise, I never thought that Bubbles would hear me. She did! The first time she started in my direction, I turned on my "off" button and crouched low on the riding mower. This worked, and as my Mom was just walking through the yard, she followed Mom. The second time, the same procedure. Then there was the third time! She came over, sat down in a nearby flower bed, and seemingly smiled, "I know it's you, there's no use pretending!"

A week or so later, Rick my nephew next door, took out the lawn mower and started to mow their lawn. Bubbles waddled over, " Ha Ha, I got you this time." She immediately saw that it was not I. "Oh well, we all make mistakes", and quickly changed the subject, and went looking for insects in the garden.

Baby Bubbles at Arianne's

We're off to the Voluntary Service Unit Meeting.

Bubbles and I at work

Mom and Bubbles

Bubbles checking out the wisk

Bubbles at her buffet 197

I was amazed at her vision, perception, and hearing. I had managed to get past her and was towing the push lawn mower at the wind break, which is a fair distance from the house. She spotted me, I froze trying to look like one of the trees. She thought I did that very poorly!

She used one tone of babbling for ordinary conversation, and another for exciting events, like not having seen me all day, or when cuddling up to me or sitting on my lap – her favourite – and a very distinct call, "Mother, where are you?" If we had been outside together and either she or I wandered off, she would call.

This sketch was drawn by Bret, one of my children in care. We were on our way to Sick Kids Hospital, Toronto.

I always answered her. If I was in the house, I would call through the screen door or window, and that would suffice, she would either continue to do her thing, which was catching insets in the garden or go to her private pool.

On August 26, she left at 9 a.m. Evening came and she did not return. Sunday evening she was back. What a "night on the town" that must have been!

She was dead tired and her tail feathers in disarray. Her 'mother' failed to tell her not to land in the tall bull-rushes, which are up to six feet tall in the large swamp just south of the house. We felt that what she had done, was landed in the rushes, and then dropped through the rushes and had to walk out of the huge swamp. Sunday noon, we had a family picnic lunch in the yard which probably helped her get orientated. She was so tired, she wanted to go to bed, to the little tool shed on the yard, without our usual ritual. For two days, she just napped on her pool.

She was not allowed in the house (for obvious reasons) during the day. At dusk she could come in. She would sit on newspapers at my feet. When she was more or less full grown, she started to object to being caught, so we put her in the tool shed for the night. To catch her we would skid over the waxed floor. I would then put her on my knee and there she would sit and bubble bedtime stories to me.

Then on a Wednesday as I drove in, she was flying up the driveway – she had learned her aviation lessons well, I thought. She circled around the house, circled the field behind the house and headed for the creek. I called, "Bubbles, where are you going?" and she circled back and crash landed close to me, between the brick flower bed wall, the watering can, and the flowers! I did suggest to her that she needed to improve her landing technique.

One evening, I decided I would give her some vacation ideas. We walked – yes walked – both of us, to the dug-out about a quarter mile from the house. She stuck to me like glue. I was excited when we got to the pond. SHE just observed. To create some enthusiasm, "like ducks take to water", on her part, I swished my hand in the water. Her observation was "yes, you're right – it's water". That was the extent of her involvement.

Bubbles arch enemy was my hoe – she would at times attack it. I felt this was jealousy on her part.

She did have the upper hand, as far as Freddie, our cat was concerned. It was made very clear to Freddie, early in Bubbles life that she was out-of-bounds for him, and

Bubbles, what a night out that was!

Shed in which Bubbles spent the nights

if he must look, it had to be at a respectable distance. Bubbles seemed to sense this priority. One day she caught me playing with Freddie near the house. She immediately waddled over to me. Freddie, taking his training seriously, streaked from the area.

Bubbles was getting very restless. She would call with a loud 'squawk', or another loud sound for which I have no translation. The only response she would hear was our imitation, or laughter! Her next-of-kin (I think) swam in the aforementioned dug-out and there were often ducks calling on the creek near by.

Good to the last drop and that is good too. Bubbles on her private pool

On September 3, at dawn, with a loud "Quack", Bubbles took off from her pond just outside my bedroom window. For the last little while she had refused to stay in the shed at night, she wanted to sleep on her pool. I did not agree, because the pool is so small, the raccoons might get her.

I wish her all the best and will diligently look for her return, next spring.

The next time that I saw her, or at least could identify her, was in early spring, of 1979, at 6:30 a.m., I was outside on the driveway mixing sprays to dormant spray some fruit trees. I heard the whistling wings of low flying ducks, looked up and saw a pair of mallard ducks flying low up our driveway. Like any good mother, I was very excited about her homecoming, dropped what I had in my hands and waved my arms, calling "Bubbles, Bubbles". The male duck, in great haste, veered off to the right and could not get away fast enough. With something that noisy, he was not taking any chances. The female duck did not alter her course or height, what so ever, but flew straight over top of me.

The summer of 1983, same hayfield, same mower, my brother Helmut said there was a mallard duck nesting just a bit behind the house.

My brother saw the nest in time this time, and left a large island of uncut grass to protect the nest. The female duck was very tame and I was sure it was Bubbles.

One day as I went to visit her, I was not talking to her as I usually did, as I was testing if this was Bubbles, and she flushed, I stopped and called "Bubbles, Bubbles". Her response was "That's mother calling, now what do I do!" She landed in the field, a short distance away, and I left.

Auf wieder sehen, Bubbles.

Bubbles sitting on her nest of a clutch of 10 eggs
June 1983

Bubbles clutch of eggs

Bubbles flushing from her nest

The Story of BUBBLY

Baby Bubbly

It was Thursday, April 18, 1991 I went to look for the "goose egg" which, Helmut my brother next door, said was laying on the pond bank. I figured the raccoons would have had it for a midnight snack by now, since he had told me about it a couple of days ago. Well it was still there. It is not a goose egg. It is blue/green, it's a mallard duck egg.

May 16 My nurse friend Marg , visited me, and said " are you trying to fry the egg". Well it worked.

I was surprised that although it was about the same size as a chicken egg, it was much heavier. I took it home and laid it on the bench outside the back door. In the evening I decided I would not leave it there for the opossum to mess around with, so I put it in the greenhouse. Well, it was the beginning of summer '91. SUN SUN SUN. During the day it was very hot in the greenhouse, but would cool off nicely during the night.

On Saturday April 20th, I decided I would put the egg under my plant lights upstairs in my bedroom. At first I thought, Oh I can do this for 3 weeks. After two weeks I thought, well just one more week to go. Then it hit me. This is a duck egg, not a chicken egg. This is a 4 week stint!

At this point in time I was on holidays from work. Since I was in my bedroom more than I would normally have been, I could keep close tabs on the temperature. Every time I was in the bedroom, I would check the temperature of the egg with my hand and move it to a hotter or cooler spot as I felt necessary. The egg was in a small box, with a straw lining in the bottom.

When I broke the news to Mom, that I had put a duck egg under the plant lights upstairs, and was trying to hatch it, Mom's response was "Oh No, the back steps!" Bubbles, in 1978, had used the back steps as her favorite parking spot.

OH NO

Every week, Saturdays to be exact, I watered the plants, and you guessed it, also the egg, straw and all. I watered it well so that the straw would be damp for a day or so.

On Wednesday, May 15, I thought well I wonder how my rotten egg is doing. I gently shook it to confirm that it was rotten, but it would not gargle, so I listened to it and could not believe my ears. **THE EGG WAS PULSATING**! It had a heart beat.

I sped over to my brother Helmut's house next door, and informed them of the good news, I was expecting – a duck.

Thursday for lunch I was invited to my friend Penny in St Catharines. I came home early after noon, and had another unusual experience. As I came hurrying into the room talking to the egg of course, when I entered the room the chick made some very excited calls, and struggled so hard that the egg rocked considerably. This was for a few moments and then it was completely quiet. The egg was piped. (The chick had broken the outer shell.) I just left it and did something else for a while. Then I went to check up again. In the next hour, the chick was completely silent. This worried me since, of course, I did not know how long he had struggled before I got home. Since I never dreamt that the egg was developing and that it would hatch, I had a very guilty conscience, about my watering practices, and that the membrane in the egg was so dried out that the chick could not break it. So I decided to operate. I gently opened a hole through the egg shell, at the piped area and also broke the membrane just a small hole, and left it for about a half hour. There was no calling or motion what so ever. So I decided that I would hatch the chick. When I opened the egg, and attempted to take the chick out, I noticed that the egg sack had not all been absorbed, so I left the back part of the egg shell intact.

Bubbly pried out of the shell – he was too weak to get out. May 16. I only watered the plants and the egg once a week, and that was not enough to keep the membrane soft. He could not break out of the egg, so I had to cut him out. (Out West Mom would sprinkle the eggs with water, when the hen was incubating them.)

I then went to visit my Mom in the Vineland Home. When I came back the little chick could not lift its head although the feet were traveling.

Next morning it was the same. I thought it had a problem with its neck, so I gave it a gentle message. (Ever try to find a chick's neck to message it!) At noon, no change, so I decided to force feed it. I got some Cream of Wheat, mixed it with water, rather runny, put it in a dropper and fed the tiny, fuzzy chick. Friday evening I was delighted, the chick was walking around in that tiny box, very normal. But being a good mother I force fed it again. I surmised that the chick was so weak from struggling to get out of the egg it was too weak to lift its head. Well, what should I name our new family member. *Why not BUBBLY.* The first duck in 1978 was BUBBLES. So what's left, BUBBLER, and BUBBLING.

Baby Bubbly, cuddling under foster mom's "wings" a bunch of kleenex. He thought Mom was a little drafty. June 1

Saturday, on my way to get Mom home for the week end, I stopped in at the local feed store. No, they had no duck starter or chick starter, and Monday was a holiday. So guess what, I resorted to good old Quaker Oats. That's what Mom and Dad had us fed a little minnow that we found alive among all the dead ones, in the frozen Wilson Lake, Sask., cattle watering hole!! Both times it worked very well.

One day in May as I was working in the flower bed along the driveway, Bubbly of course was close by. When I was beating a clay lump trying to get it to conform, Bubbly hurried over and ate some of that dirt and YUK! He spit it out. Bubbly thought I was calling/showing him some delicate morsel. He had noticed on other occasions that "Mom" seemed a bit off base!!

May 18 Baby Bubbley telling me a story

Bubbly bubbling in his water May 20,

What'ca doing Ma May 29

I'm doing the evening paper

Hey Ma, let's go for a waddle

I think I'll go

Our Out Tripping:

The Supervisor Trudy, asked us to come for a visit. Our first trip, was to the Vineland Home, I took Bubbly for show and tell. He was hatched on May 16. I set him on the floor and he would follow me as if he were on an elastic "Sure a lot of feet with white shoes around here!" and it did get a bit confusing with all those white shoes, ouuuing and aaaaaawing.

On June 1 Bubbly had a crash course in independence. At this point in time we could not tell the sex of the fuzzy yellow and brown down covered chick. We would have to wait till it got feathers. He was confined in a little chicken wire enclosure, which had a hole where he could get out.

In this way I hoped to have him be aware of his whereabouts and find his way back. Sure. When I looked out, he was nowhere in sight but I could hear him calling. I went out and called it out of the neighbors – across our common driveway – flower bed. I had put out his night box, on its side, complete with foster mom – Kleenex – hanging up so he could cuddle under them, and an oven grate partly covering the front. Since he was having real pangs of independence for the last few days, we waddled to the box which was also accompanied by his pool and food. When he tried to streak past me, which I knew he would try, I steered him into the box. I went in the house he climbed the stairs, best he could, like climbing up the astilbe plant and onto the next step. He then decided to check the other side of the house, where he promptly got caught in a

Bubbly was not only well read, but also well travelled – we're off to the Vineland Home, to visit Mom. May 23.

Bubbly in his cat-proof enclosure June 21,

That's got to go

Bubbly studying his GPS June 2

Amos and Annie – Amos was tame and impulsive, Annie was squirrelly. June 12 1985

pile of fruit tree netting. I heard him call for help, got him untangled and again did the box run. I went in the house again. He now had caught on. He went to the food and pool then went in the box for a siesta. Later in the day I again put him into the wire pen, since I would be gone till early evening and I didn't trust our "pride" of cats.

To night I let him out after doing some lawn cutting. He did his stroll and then hung around the food and box. **What a bright little Bubbly. After 2 lessons, he had it down pat.**

It would have taken Amos & Annie – two squirrels that I raised – "a month of Sundays" to catch on!

In early June his first feathers showed on his wings, followed by his first 'Quack', "MOM, where are you?"

Duck, my third language.

Starting to get wing-feathers.

The Teenager

That's cool!

Our first parent/teenage struggle. He walked into the house and instead of going into his box (he is not house trained) he zipped into the back bedroom. I zipped after him, caught him, and **walked** him to his box. **He never pulled that stunt again.** He did not want me to hold him. It's a deal, you obey the rules, and I don't catch.

One day the short-haired dark calico cat came from the barn, not even a glance at the duckling, did not even think of glazed duck, but went straight to the cistern high

Hey wait for me. You try walkig a mile in my shoes
August

Boots, one of our kitties.

A yard scene

Bubbly bubbling on the driveway

Bubbly telling Mom and I everything he has done this morning,

Let me tell you what I just did

Bub Powering Up "Just look at those wings!" I never saw Bubbles do this. The day that I was going to teach her how to fly, she could not waddle as fast as I walked, then she just flew!

Generating muscles

And like this

And July 1

I can also so stretch them one at a time

perch to look for mice in the tall grass below it. "No matter what it looks like, it's part of our family!"

On June 22 and 23 Mom was home after 2 weeks not at home. On numerous occasions Bubby would come to the door calling and chatting, assuming I was talking to him. I live alone, don't usually talk to myself that loud.

It's the beginning of July, and Bubbly was very restless, working hard on his fully grown wings, calling – but not me.

Also did a Quack call this morning. He might not know that I'm not a duck, but he sure knows he is, and is working out his long wings often and hard.

Bubbly and I started to waddle to the south dug out, by the creek. We no sooner got started, when in a distance, high in the sky a red-tailed hawk was drifting on the thermals. This did not bypass Bubbly's keen eye sight. Bubbly refused to continue. I refused to give up. (Another child parent encounter) I caught Bubbly and proceeded towards the pond. I wanted to give him some holiday ideas, and here he could also socialize with ducks that looked more like him. The field I was walking in had the second cut of hay off, along side a field of standing corn, so it was easy going. Bubbly was protesting for all he was worth, about two pounds. I put him down, and in deafening silence he made a bee-line into the tall corn. A few yards in that and he realized it was not a wise decision, so he came out, headed straight for home. Oh well, then so did I. You win some and you loose some!

The ducks hangout

What did you say? June

The barn AND the road

One of the flower beds on the yard

July 15 was his 1st flight, he flew in the apple orchard from where I was coming from spraying, about 10 – 15 feet and landed near me. Then a few days later his 2ⁿ flight, flying behind Helmut's house east, then back along the road and landed on the driveway again.

Another power struggle coming up. I had planned to train him to go to the south dug- out, there we did not have to cross the highway. But, ducks have an excellent memory, **(if some one calls me 'Bird Brain'**, *I say thank you!)* so I headed for the recent dug-out from which we get our water for the barn, behind the barn. A highway goes right through our yard. The two houses are on the south side of the road, and the barns, sheds, cows, cats etc are on the north side. We all seem to have the joggers pace! Bubbly came as far as the highway, stood on it and appeared to think "this is pretty good, it's easy walking, good visibility, if only I could swim here" Being a 50 MPH zone, Mom did not have much time to explain. I caught Bubbly and carried him to the dug out, right to the edge of the water.

I think this plant needs shaping June

He is very cautious in new situations. After a few minutes he proceeded to go to a shallow spot and bubble around in the water. The banks of the dug-out are very steep, he threaded his way down, ran/flew a few yards into the water and scampered back to shore. Since it was getting late and Bubbly thought he may want to stay awhile, I chased him home.

Bubbly bubbling my sandal

The Adult

Most people sneak into the house – I out! In the morning of Saturday July 20, after letting him out of the house, I refilled his dish with duck starter (spoiled – would you say!) and managed to sneak around the house past the far side of the east flower bed, and across the road to the barn. I wanted to get some natural goodness, fertilizer, for my cacti in the greenhouse. I had no sooner started to fill my bottle when Bubbly flew by me and landed, with that "lets go to the pond idea" in his head. At this point we're half way there, so we waddled the rest of the way through a first-cut hay field, a bit bumpy for big feet and short legs.

You try walking in that tall grass with shoes like this!

Bubbly at his buffet

Ma look what I can do!

You can't see me!

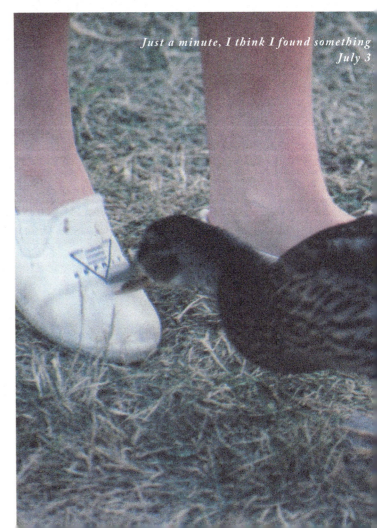
Just a minute, I think I found something
July 3

Coming Ma

Ker Choooo

    This time he did not want to go where we were on Friday, he wanted a short cut. I waited for a few minutes, told him I was leaving and started off, humming. He stayed and I was pleased he did. Early afternoon I went to the pond, humming. No sign of Bubbly, I went to the spot were we had been Friday and stood there for a few minutes, still no sign of him. Then I proceeded to slowly circle the pond. Yes, your right, still humming, instead of always chattering with Bubbly. I often hum so he knows where I am. He does not mind what I hum! All of a sudden out of the reeds on the opposite side, out comes Bubbly.

    He flew a few feet above the water, and since the water level is down considerably he did not land where he had hoped. He flew, ran in the water back and forth until he could get out of the water. I guess Mom must have missed a page or two in duck Dr Spock. Anyways, he decided to stay there and not come to the more slanting area. I left humming. Got my camera and went back. He was still where I had left him. I took a picture of him and he decided he would join me. Well, instead of taking a picture were Bubbly is flying straight for me, I was urging him, ***"Bubbly, Bubbly, up higher, higher, you have to clear a fence"***. He did, and we waddled home.

    Sunday morning he thought I owed him one. No I'm not going to the pond this morning. He would hang around the steps and door calling. After lunch, he needed no coaching, we trundled off to the pond. I got hot just watching him walk. I left him at the pond area and went back. Before Fasba, coffee break, I said to Mom I will just slip over to the pond and see if Bubbly wants to come home. I got out the door, and Bubbly came to meet me, "rather a long nap you had wasn't it?" He was very chatty and very happy to be back. Mother and I sat on the back step chatting, and he came to challenge mother's right to visit with me.

    Later in the evening I took Mom back to the Home.

Tickle Tickle Aug. 5

I didn't tickle your toes

*You called?
In his loving stance*

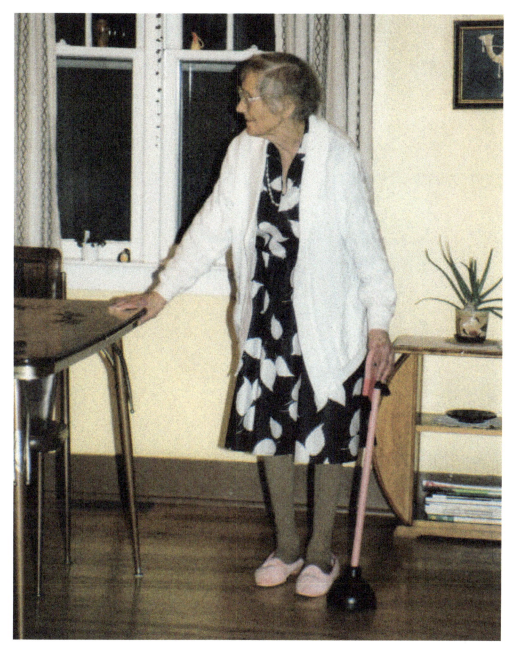

Mom and her multi purpose walking cane.

Bubbly followed the car, flying to the end of the driveway. I took off like a "teenager" two wheels on the shoulder to make a lot of dust and he quit following.

When I got back it was rather dark already. He was not on the yard, so I hurried, humming, to the pond. When I got to our spot, I just stood and listened, and very close by someplace in the reeds, Bubbly was chattering away with that "I'm very pleased with myself" chatter. I knew that he was happy and left.

Oh Bubbly to your box!

No Bubbly, no sight seeing, straight to your box July

Should I just make a run for it. Into your box Bubbly

Or just dash this way?

***BOY**, Mom's in a raw mood tonight*

His first night spent on the Pond.

Too hot to work in the sun now

The following day, early in the morning, I slipped over to the pond. Bubbly was swimming in the middle of the 17 foot deep pond and when he saw me he started to show off. He up-ended, such a familiar sight with mallards feeding in SHALLOW water. Their tail is up, their head is down, pulling weeds etc. When he could not reach anything, he dove. Mallards usually do not dive. I knew it, he didn't. He was very happy and relaxed in the water. I wondered whether other ducks spent the night there too.

Latter I started working out side, it was as cool as it would be for a while. I was setting up a perennial hardy cacti bed. I was making good progress, no one biting my toes, checking for bugs between my feet and sandals, challenging my gloves to the right to hold weeds etc. At one point I had the urge to look up and guess who was standing there and looking at me? When I spoke to him, he had the very loving and humble, friendly pose, curved neck, low stance and told me all about his night out!

Since he had been with me all morning and not gone back to the pond, I decided I would go to the pond and then past the pond to glean some wheat which the combine would have left, for a bouquet. Well, I lived through the task of taking him across the road, **Again**. He stopped on the road and reminisced about all the potential, as about four cars went swishing by. He did not budge, just kind of thought, "watch it you guys, aren't you coming a little too close!!". We went to the pond, he stayed and I gleaned some wheat. When I returned past the pond, Bubbly came waddling along too. **Oh yes the road**. As we neared the road, I tried to build up Bubbly's momentum to improve

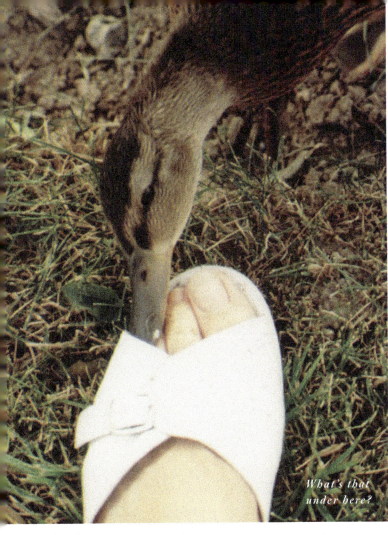
What's that under here?

Mom has various shaped feet

Speech Speech – in his loving stance

There seems to be an extra piece here

Gotta see if the plant needs water

I am thinking tonight of my Blue eyes, and I wonder .....

Look Ma, I can stand on one foot August 20,

I can also do it with my other foot

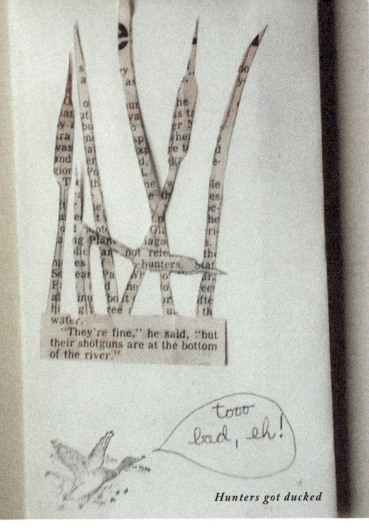

"They're fine," he said, "but their shotguns are at the bottom of the river."

tooo bad, eh!

Hunters got ducked

I wonder where the rest of Mom is?

Helmut's little rubber duck. FAKE. That's not funny,

Hey Ma, let's go for a walk

Now where should I go? The Mallard ducks are know as the Dabblers. It is often seen in the tipped-up position, with it's tail held vertical. They feed in shallow water, that is all except Bubbly,

Bubbly chatting with one of his favorite companions Aug. 5

Out Bubbly July

OK OK, I'm going

AND she says I'm grouchy

his timing across the road. <u>You guessed it. It was off.</u> He did not break waddle when he finally did get there just as this hydro truck was approaching. The driver saw Bubbly waddling to the road and my babbling at Bubbly. He stopped the truck and had a good laugh. So much for the escorted waddle to the pond.

Bubbly took great offense, if you pushed him out of the way with your foot. After this he would often attach my foot off and on. Today I could not break him of this. I finally caught him and dumped him in the pond – he was in such a raw mood. He was back at dark, sulking, would not chatter with me, but wanted in the house. I won some and I lost some – encounters. He spent the night in the house.

The next morning was the first time that he did not greet me immediately, he did after a few minutes. July 27 Saturday – 2nd night on the pond. Sunday after noon two large dogs stopped in. Bubbly took off from the back door steps to the pond and stayed there the night.

This is his territory. He flew back to protect his clothes line area. Aggressive little Bubbly Aug. 24

Bubbly happy and content in his box, with his bill through the grate, near to me,

Yes I pecked at her, now I'll just wait a minute to see how she'll respond. His bill not through the grate.

Bubbles and Bubbly meet

July 29 Monday, in the a.a.m. (before breakfast) I went to the barn yard and got a wheel barrel of soil for the herb bed. There among the cows, was an old female mallard, waddling around, catching flies or whatever ! She must have heard and seen me long before I noticed her. I don't usually look for ducks among the cows! When I first noticed her, I was reasonably close. At first glance I thought it must be Bubbly, but then noticed immediately it was not. It was an old female mallard – drab dull colouring. **OLD BUBBLES**!!!! ***I was stunned, so I said "Bubbles is that you."*** I did not know what else to say!

This is where I first , again, saw Old Bubbles, walking among the cows in the barn yard Aug. 24, 1991

Old Bubbles at the back, and Bubbly leading the way

She looked up, continued to feed and then in no great haste, she flew up, circled a trifle and left. Could her mother not have told her that mallard ducks don't hang out with cows! In the evening, Bubbly was very pushy/demanding to come into the house for the night.

August 3, Saturday, this morning while getting the cows in from the barnyard Helmut walked up to Old Bubbles, to about 10 feet. She looked scruffy, gave a quack and flew off. Later that evening Helmut did not see Old Bubbles, flushed her, she flew up and landed a little further in the yard. He came and told me, I went out, but she was gone. Cows probably had chased her. When I arrived in the barn yard Bubbly arrived also, we waddled across the barn yard, only two older dry cows there, and then to the pond to see if Bubbles was there. No she was not.

DUCK LIVES – (more than cats!!)

During my Sunday afternoon nap, two cars blew their horns. Later during the week – BRaaaaaaaaaaaaaaaaakkkkkkeeeeesssss !!!!

In early August I took pictures of OLD BUBBLES in the barnyard. Later in the week, the men folk, who had gone to the barn earlier, said Bubbly was visiting with pigeons on the barn yard. Oh well, I guess as long as they can fly.

Early this morning I took my camera and went to look for Old Bubbles. (Helmut and son Rick had seen her in the barnyard) She was not there now. Bubbly came flying from the house, past me and flew to the pond. I walked to the pond, chatted a few seconds with Bubbly who was on the far shore, and as I turned to leave, he flew and joined me. He struggled through the longish grass for a while, then decided, not me, I'm flying back to the pond. Shortly after I left for work, Old Bubbles and Bubbly arrived on the drive way. Old Bubbles then flew south up the driveway, Bubbly did too but circled the houses and came back to the driveway.

One afternoon as I was working at home, due to my bite lip (had been to the dentist – it had been frozen and I bit, hard) Bubbles and Bubbly were on the yard until I hollered to Bubbly and asked where he'd been. Bubbly was near the picnic table. I went to the door to go out, and had not seen Bubbles at the pump and she flew off.

In the evening Bubbles and Bubbly paraded along the driveway to the road. Inge, Helmut's wife, from next door, escorted Bubbly back from the road on one side of the driveway, while Old Bubbles waddled along on the other side.!! Helmut took this pictures.

A mid August evening Bubbly hung around the door while I was in the house making jam. He had been on the steps since 7:45 p.m. At 8:30 he was very willing to come in. I worked in the kitchen till 9 p.m. Bubbly was very annoyed, nipped at me when I went by his box. His soother/bed time story is I sit at the table with my foot at his cage grate and he sits next to my foot. He bit my slipper, I showed him the sole, which he takes as a VERY aggressive gesture on my part. He then, as usual, pushed my foot with his beak and head. That's some two and a half pounds of push, but does not send me spinning. I put my foot down by the grate in a peaceful park, he promptly buried his aggression and sat down next to it.

When he is annoyed at me he comes with neck arched, and bill down and is silent. He also has this posture when he feels very happy, only then he chatters. One evening as Helmut left my house, with his water jug, he called back, "Bubbly thinks you are a bank, he just left a deposit!" Oh No!

In mid August I started Bubbly on grain – bird seed – he loved it. Last evening Bubbly went to the pond. I had snuck out to the machine shop and was talking to Helmut. Bubbly knew I was there, waited on the driveway then took off. He had been very unhappy the previous night, because I continued to work in the kitchen while he was pining away, alone, in his box. This evening it's Bubby in the box again. Bubbly sat at the well till dark twilight, then came to the door and asked to come in. Was in a horrible mood. Eventually his nipping my foot turned to rough attacks and I took up the challenge. I showed him the bottom of my slipper. He went crazy, pecking and pushing up against the grate and my slipper for all he was worth. (have to ask the druggist how much! – Humans $? Ducks $?..) He started thrusting his head through the upper space in the grate and got his head caught. That really upset and humbled him, and nursed his head ache for a few minutes. Then he sat close to my foot and settled right down, with just his beak out of the grate as usual. **He is so bright, but with a streak of stubbornness**. At one point he made a quick tap on my foot, sat with his beak behind the grate for a few seconds, waiting to see what my response would be, and then again rested his beak outside the grate.

This evening after I came home and feed him, he flew up the driveway, above and in front of Helmut who was walking from the machine shop to the barn, banked between the buildings and flew to the pond. (for ten minutes) **Helmut called "I ducked that one!"**

It's evening and I'm in "Duck-House" again. Bubbly was angry that I carried a new ladder in his territory. He's not speaking to me. Mum's, the word. After supper I spoke to him and he had forgiven me and was chattering again. Latter that evening I quite working outside, fed Bubbly grain and went in. He ate, came towards the door, went back and ate. Called. I was very quiet, (did not even talk to myself) at 8:06 p.m., the sun was already low in the sky, Bubbly took off north on the driveway to the road, east along the road, then towards behind the heifer barn, north east, and west across the barn yard to the pond. Hope he spends the night there. He did. I was trying to encourage him to spend the night on the pond, with the other ducks.

Old Bubbles not sure who it is, and takes off.

Old Bubbles, That's Mom calling! Aug

Hi Mom! wasn't sure it was you

On this Sunday, since he not at the house by 8;30 a.m. I went to the pond to see if they both were on the water. They both – for sure. I did not see Bubbles, she flushed and flew further into the pond and swam, I called her, she stopped, turned around and swam a few yards back toward me, stopped, thought, and then took off west.

Bubbly did not know whether to follow her or me, he waddled after me. Helmut said that both Bubbly and Bubbles had been feeding in the barnyard earlier, but not together.

I noticed yesterday that Bubbly is all grey underneath and today I saw that he has many tiny rust feathers on his chest, and a few emerald green feathers on his head. **Bubbly is a male**.

One evening I went to see if Old Bubbles was in the pond too. Bubbly was in the pond along the north reeds. He wanted to come to me, would start and stop. I had not said a word. I left. He flew and joined me and we waddled back – my fault he stays in the house tonight. I picked beans at late dusk, and he was happily chasing bugs.

He wanted to leave and fly back to the pond, it was just the last light going, he would see me and come back towards the house. I actively did not show myself, and he left for the pond at about 8:45 p.m.

When I have company in the evening he feels I am talking to him (like usual) and he does not fly to the pond for the night. In the box tonight. Tonight it was full moon

I was weeding in the garden, when I came upon this bunny nest of young. I rushed away from the area, and Bubbly was wondering why I was leaving in such a hurry, he had not seen them, but he sensed there was something very interesting here, but he follow me out.

I can't change feet like that

– a duck flew around the greenhouse west to east, past my bedroom window, calling. I called and went to the door. No Bubbly.

Late August, Bubbly and I in a power struggle again. I was standing behind the machine shop waiting for him to come and look for me and we would waddle to the pond. He was on the driveway, staring me down. After a while I gave up, it was getting dark, I came around the machine shop just as he started to fly towards the road and me. A car came just then, and he was swooped over the car about by a foot. He flew into the weeds and started running in a daze, wings hanging. He did not touch the car. I caught him and checked his wings. They were ok. At first he did not struggle. After a while, while walking to the pond, he started to struggle a bit. I popped him into the pond. **He was in shock.** I felt he would be more relaxed in the pond, than picking an argument with me, while in his box in the house.

Early next morning I checked on him. He was swimming a bit in the pond, but was confused. When I called him he was afraid and headed for the reeds. I went closer, he could hardly push the reeds aside while swimming, he was so very weak. I was out of town for two day, and when I got back I immediately check on Bubbly. I just went to the pond and sang, stood at my usual spot, but no sign of Bubbly. ***I was afraid he had been un-imprinted.*** In the evening I took my binoculars and searched for Bubbly from my usual spot, at first quietly, then I started to call. Then there was a loud splash, as if he was taking off from the water, but no, nothing. After a while I started walking around the pond checking the rushes. *There he was, not a feather out of place, floating dead on the water in the reed area from which he often flew to me. He had died from shock.*

Bub is dead in the pond

After I went to bed, I thought again about Bubbly, I was sad and also in a way relieved. The splash I heard was Bubbly starting to come to me, because Mom was calling. <u>He was not un-imprinted</u>!

A few days later, very early in the morning, Old Bubbles flew by and was calling Bubbly, just south of the house. *She missed Bub too!*

In mid October, late dusk, Helmut and I had been talking on the driveway. I went to cover cactus #99 – still outside – Helmut went to put out the shop lights. A duck was flying a short distance behind the house calling!! I called "Bubbles", but she continued on her way. **LOVE YOU BUBBLES!**

1992 – Next Year – after Bubbly

In late April as I got home from Church, I saw Bubbles, mating in the water filled ditch in the wheat field behind the house, the field in which she was born.

Later during the week when I came home from work in the evening, Bubbles and Beau were along the road, in a water filled ditch on our road, just west of the horse barn. The female was splashing around enjoying life. The male was nervously parading along the bank of the ditch. In early June 24th, Bubbles flew low – 15 feet – over the drive way towards the barn. I had seen a lone duck fly over the farm a few days before, a little higher.

Old Bubbles courting, in the field behind the house, where she was born Sept. 1992

1993 – 2nd year – after Bubbly

In mid June, Helmut and I were unloading baled hay. Helmut said he saw a tame duck sitting on the tire, floating in the pond. He drove by quite close and she didn't pay any attention to him. After we finished the load, Helmut circled out with the wagon, back of the barnyard, beside the pond, and got a second load, Old Bubbles was still there. After unloading the second load at 5:30 p.m., I got my camera and went to the pond, addressing her by name as I approached. She stayed put, after a while she got up and stretched and walked around to the other side of the tire. I then left, talking as I went, so she knew where I was. At 9 p.m. as I was finishing working in the veggy garden, three ducks were flying and arguing, like they have for weeks. I always called " Bubbles" when I saw them zipping back and forth, wondering if Bubbles was one of them. She was not part of that Trika. Just after I finished calling to them, a lone duck came flying from behind the barn, low over the tool shed, over the garden, just about over me and off to the Creek.! (***Dear Old Bubbles – who was 15 years young on June 27, 1993***)

Old Bubbles gets up and stretches

Old Bubbles being friendly. July 1994 @ age 16 – Our last picture of Old Bubbles

Dad and Mom's first home was on the Prairie, Hanley, Sk. Dad called this picture "When I and You were Young Maggie"

SIR BUBBLY July 20, 1991

My family in Struan. Back row: Dad, Hilda, Mom Front row: Lydia, Helmut, Nelly

Our first house in Struan

1994 – 3rd year, after Bubbly

On April 24 at dusk, Helmut and I are talking on the drive way. Two ducks flew up the driveway over us relatively low. (**Guess Who** !) A few days later Inge saw Bubbles and Beau grazing just south of their lawn.

In late August I was driving on Chippawa Creek Road just west of Wilson's house, Bubbles and Beau were feeding along the ditch!! The female was relaxed and feeding, the male was a nerves wreck, "Do you have to feed so close to people traffic !"

On August 31, @ 8:35 p.m. it was cloudy & dark, Helmut said that as he shut the shed doors, he heard a "Quack Quack" over head! *Old Bubbles said 'Good Night'.*

Bubbles and I had few disagreements, while Bubbly and I had scores of them. I have told my family, I need to raise another mallard, to figure out why such very different behaviors between the two Kids. Which was personality, and which was gender related!!

Old Bubbles was last seen in August 1994. She was born June 27, 1978. That made her 16 years old. The Creek is just south of the houses, and every fall a lot of hunters, hunt in the marsh. She has dodged the bullets for 16 years. **Way to go Bubbles**.

What a JOY she and Bubbly were to the whole family.

According to a report from the U.S.A Fish and Wildlife, the Mallard Duck maximum life span can be –

14 years (shot) U.S.
16 years(shot) Russia
29 years (found dead) U.S.

CPSIA information can be obtained
at www.ICGtesting.com
Printed in the USA
LVOW06s0321260416
485288LV00020B/92/P